28 Days to A Better Marriage

Advice on how you can have the relationship with your spouse that you've always wanted.

Dale Sadler
Licensed Professional Counselor

ABOUT THE AUTHOR

Dale Sadler is a Licensed Professional Counselor, Mental Health Service Provider, School Counselor, speaker, minister, artist, fly fisherman, author, obstacle course runner, and hiker. After earning his bachelor's degree in Bible from Freed-Hardeman University, he and his wife Malita moved to Portland, TN, where he worked as a full-time youth minister. It was during this time period that he earned his master's degree in Marriage and Family Therapy from Western Kentucky University. Not long after graduating, Dale began working with the local middle school, earning his School Counselor certification and then his Professional Counseling license.

In 2010, Dale received the top honor at the Tennessee School Counselors and Administrator's Institute where he has been a regular presenter. His blog, "In Search for More" (www.insearchformore.com) was named one of the top fifty blogs for marriage advice by MastersInCounseling.com. His writings have been featured in *Think Magazine*, the "Newsletter for the Tennessee Association of Marriage and Family Therapy," *Kaio* (a Christian Magazine for teens), the website for the National Center for Fathering, *Church Growth*, and he is a regular blogger for EmpoweringParents.com. He is also published regularly in local newspapers. Dale is an active member with the International Association of Marriage and Family Counselors.

At his private practice in White House, TN, Dale specializes in marriage, parenting, and men's issues. He enjoys working with families and married couples. Dale believes that most families can thrive, and those who aren't, have either forgotten or just don't know how. Oftentimes, the members of the family or marriage are simply doing all the wrong things and this is what causes their turmoil. Dale can help both groups learn to function properly and rediscover the joy of being together. Also, while many men could benefit from counseling, they are typically reluctant to seek it. Dale wants to help men everywhere be the best for their wives, their children, and themselves.

If you are interested in Dale speaking to your church or group, his seminar, *Eden Again: Bringing Paradise Back to Marriage* uses a scientifically proven assessment, humor, and other proven strategies to get your couples excited about their marriage.

Find Dale on Facebook or Twitter @DaleSadlerLPC. Also, visit his website to subscribe to his blog, e-zine, or to read more about his work as a counselor and speaker. Also, be sure to check out Dale's other Kindle book, *How to Argue with Your Teen and Win: Tactics for Communicating More Effectively with Your Child.*

www.DaleSadler.net

Table of Contents

Day 1

Let's Get to Work

The story of when you first fell in love is probably a beautiful one that you could tell really well. You know where you were, what you were doing, and probably even what you were wearing; at least what he or she was wearing. It was a powerful moment. I know mine was. Although, let's face it, when we say, "fall in love," what we really mean is that a deep level of infatuation took us over when we saw THAT person. While we couldn't sleep or eat for days and all we could do was think about him or her, it was not really love. You see this is part of the problem. We consider love too frivolously. How can what we feel in a magical moment carry us for fifty years? It can't. This is why love must be taken more seriously and understood for what it is.

While love is not a hole we fall into, it is a place that we often work our way out of because of a lack of commitment. Think you'll be happier with that other person? Think again. He or she has just as many (if not more) personal problems and annoyances as your current spouse. Think that other person will be pleasant in the morning? Think again. He may be just as grumpy. Think that other person won't leave her towels on the floor? Think again. She may not pull the curtain in during her shower leaving the floor completely wet.

You see, these are the things that drive us crazy but that can only be seen when living with someone and that are totally missed when you don't. Stop focusing on the little things that bother you and start looking for and making the good. It will revolutionize your relationship.

For the last six years my taxes have been processed by the same accountant. I like visiting him. We talk about each other's kids and in a strange way, he's been watching my kids grow up. We don't talk on Facebook, email or converse in any other social way, but twice per year we'll have a great meeting with one another. Maybe it's because I get a return. Who knows? What I do know is that this relationship is easy to maintain. I see him for about two hours and he gives me good news.

Some relationships aren't this way. Two people who are madly in love with each other get married and soon thereafter get a divorce. Some would say that this means that marriage is obsolete. Well, I don't blame the institution; I blame those who don't have a firm grasp on what marriage is.

Marriage is no longer "you and I." It is us, and "us" means that I must bend not break. I must think before I speak and I must be composed when I want to yell. It means sharing the good with someone special and because they are so special you know that there is nothing that is so bad that you would want to leave him/her. That would be devastating. It means you will work to be at your best because he/she will do the same for you and WOW is that good! Marriage means more than just a few calls each week. It means checking in because you don't want him/her to worry.

Some relationships require very little effort. Others, especially marriage, need work and time spent on them. Nothing worthwhile ever comes easy. I hope this book is your first step in improving your marriage. Read one chapter per day and resolve to apply its wisdom.

Day 2

Don't Stay Together for the Kids

It's no surprise that the institution of marriage is in turmoil. Couples, at their marital breaking point, often choose divorce as a solution. I know that divorce is not always avoidable. However, if you are considering divorce or are just unhappy in your marriage, I hope this book can offer some insight. We must work on what we have before us rather than trading it in; especially in light of the fact that your chances of divorce increase with each subsequent marriage. The grass might be greener, but it still has to be mowed.

Divorce, under almost any circumstance, can be traumatic. Emotional devastation, added burdens, and the uncertainty of it all can send each spouse into a whirlwind taking months or even years to recover. The children also suffer from divorce. Not to be misunderstood, many single parent and step-family homes do a wonderful job with their children because of healthy modeling of what a family can be. Whatever your family looks like, it must be a positive place for sons and daughters to learn their roles as spouses and parents.

Many couples, not wanting to hurt their children, stay together. This is terribly shortsighted. Spouses who don't work on what is killing their relationship may only give their children a framework for what an unhealthy one looks like. "Just sweep it under the rug and everything will be fine." How awful! You must do more than stay together. You must work on your marriage for your children and for yourselves. Dysfunction, the inability to handle family interactions constructively, is unhealthy whether you're together or not.

One problem with a lot of marriages is that one or both spouses are not completely committed. Couples who were once passionate are now stagnant because things like money, work, and even children have skewed their perspective. Love must be nurtured over time as each partner changes and develops as a person.

Robert Fulghum, author of *Everything I Need To Know I Learned In Kindergarten*, tells the story of a culture that believes when couples argue, they are making love. In this scenario you come to a better understanding and appreciation of one another, as the conflict is resolved constructively. You are *making* love.

Some couples argue without resolution, and instead of growing together, they grow apart. The controversy must end positively for both parties, otherwise it will fester and the gloves will come out each time the subject is revisited.

If you and your spouse are at the brink of separation, you must reconnect. Send the kids to grandma's house this weekend, attend a marriage seminar, or seek counseling. You must rediscover why you first fell in love with that person and why you should love them now. Marriage is not a license to give up on each other. It's a license to have the deepest relationship possible with another human being.

Day 3

HELP! My Marriage Is In Chaos

Chaos theory is a field of study in mathematics, with applications in several disciplines including physics, economics, biology, and philosophy. I believe it also has a place in marriage theory.

Chaos theory studies the behavior of a dynamic system that is highly sensitive to its current condition. Small differences in initial conditions yield any number of widely diverging outcomes, causing chaos to result. This makes predictions nearly impossible even though the behavior of these systems (weather, the human body and marriages) can be determined by past observations and their current state.

In other words, for marriages, a small factor between a husband and wife can make an immense difference in how they interact whether for the bad or the good. Is your marriage in chaos? It might be a matter of changing a few simple things. Not to be deceiving, the change is quite difficult.

A basic part of chaos theory that one must understand is that the chaotic event that occurs did not happen at the moment of impact but rather hours, days, or weeks prior. For example, a car wreck doesn't occur just because someone runs a red light. It occurs because the person oversleeps and gets tangled up in all the effects that come from running late in the morning. Had the driver assured the clock was set and their necessary items for the morning were prepared the night before, disaster could have been averted. In marriages, a couple can have an argument hours after they see each other simply because the husband didn't hug his wife when he got in from work or she didn't greet him warmly. Not doing things for your spouse (hugging, kissing, etc) can cause a feeling of disdain to grow from literally nothing. You don't know why you're angry you just are. The nothing that has been occurring has literally eaten a dark whole in your relationship.

The movie *Blue Valentine* is a wonderfully tragic example of how marriages can live in sustained chaos. It is extremely real and I would not watch it if I was easily offended. "The film centers on a contemporary married couple, charting their evolution over a span of years by cross-cutting between time periods." (IMDb.com) You see them as a couple getting to know each other and as spouses ready to explode at any moment.

You watch as the daily stress of life and a lack of positive marital assets makes even the most normal activity a struggle. They constantly fight and it seems that this is the only thing they know how to do. Basically, life has gotten to them, they can't handle it, so they turn on one another.

Like many struggling marriages, they are stressed and want to have a good time one weekend. The wife is on call (as a nurse) and the place the husband wants to go is a good distance from their house. Many mistakes occur within this sequence that husbands could learn from. First, he asks her to go away for a weekend where she won't be able to concentrate and unwind. She's on call at the hospital and because of this will not be fully with him and therefore unable to offer what they both will want. The chaos begins. Second, once they are at the hotel, you wonder how on earth someone could pick such a tacky place. She was not impressed. Does the husband have any real idea about what the wife wants? It was like that time Homer bought Marge a bowling ball because *he* liked to bowl. Third, they turn to the alcohol to "loosen up" and all this does is make him angry and her scared, ruining the night. A chaotic event, indeed.

This type of pattern repeats itself regularly in that they can't get together on what should happen because he is oblivious and she doesn't know how to assert what she needs. Plus, if she did, he would become defensive. He wants to make it a great time; she is not mentally or emotionally there, but doesn't want to disappoint him so she goes along with it. This house of cards will not stand. By trying to force a romantic evening among bad circumstances and getting angry when the desired results don't occur, the husband finds himself in a chaotic sequence of events that he doesn't understand. Most husbands would just get angry but in this extreme case the husband, played by Ryan Gosling, turns violent.

Husbands must learn three things about their wives when

doing anything, but particularly when trying to set up a romantic evening.

First, she has to decompress from the stress of life. She can't have anything on her mind that is stressful if she is going to be the woman she knows you want her to be and that she wants to be for you. If you are a part of this stress, listen to your wife and support her in what she needs.

Men must learn what their wives need and when they need it. Men become frustrated with their wives when they are upset about something. You must respect your wife's right to feel a certain way because she's not a garbage man. Just because you put something on the street, it doesn't mean she's going to drive by and pick it up.

One evening away from the kids won't make things better if you can't enjoy regular days with your spouse. You must learn to cooperate and function like a family should. A quote from the movie really stuck with me and I hope it encourages you to get the help you need.

The wife, played by Michelle Williams, is eating dinner at her parents' home and it is obvious that her parents don't get along. While you watch this uncomfortable scene, Williams' character says the following in explaining her parents:

"I know they must have loved each other at one time. Did they just get it all out of the way before they had me? How can you trust your feelings when they just disappear like that?" The feelings don't have to disappear. You can make them come back and have the love in your marriage that you dream about.

Day 4

Do You Have A Five Star Marriage?

My wife and I recently purchased a Wii gaming system for my son. We have been reluctant to do so, but after playing with some friends we found that it can be a very good family activity.

I have played nearly every game system since Pong so I'm a pretty good game-head. However, never did I think that my prowess for games like Mortal Kombat and Mario Cart translate into the game, Just Dance 2. I suppose my days listening to Vanilla Ice in the early 90's actually paid off. Anyway, I'm good, particularly considering my size and lack of agility.

On the screen you are given a score and as your score climbs, there are stars that appear. The goal is to get 5 stars. For the first time today I noticed that the stars get progressively bigger, and after looking at the first four, one wouldn't notice unless you could compare the first to the fifth. The growth among those is so slight. It's taken a lot of work, but I can top the score every time on James' Brown's "I Feel Good." Now, if I can only get as good on Blondie's "Call Me."

The happiness in your marriage may be two stars, three stars, or even four stars, but is something keeping you from reaching that fifth star? Did you know there was such a thing? Like in the game, you may not know unless you've been there.

Did you know that you can be happy at home? Did you know that you can learn how to handle your kids? Did you know that you can go fishing and your wife actually be glad and miss you while you're gone? Did you know that you can spend money on clothes and your husband not question it? Did you know that divorce doesn't have to be the answer to your marital unhappiness?

Marriage is not always a bed of roses, but it is always a place that we can grow as individuals and as a couple. You just have to learn how to do it. I've worked with many couples who come in and then leave knowing what they should do to make their marriage better. Sometimes knowledge of what to do and how to do it is all you need.

If demands on our life are higher than our skill set, we become angry. For instance, if I put you to a task that you were unfamiliar with and asked you to do it perfectly the first time, you'd get frustrated and would do whatever you could to get away from me. However, if you spent time learning, you would become much more adept at the task and even learn to enjoy it. Commit to having a five star marriage and it just might happen.

Day 5

Why Marriage Is So Difficult

So many relationship stories begin with a beautiful tale of how a boy swept a girl off her feet. My wife's story and mine begins with brownies and continues fifteen years later with two great kids. Song of Solomon is a beautiful book in the Bible that poetically describes a man's desire for his wife. "The fig tree has ripened its figs, and the vines in blossom have given forth their fragrance. Arise, my darling, my beautiful one, and come along!'" (Song of Solomon 2:13) Try that one on her at 5am.

Unfortunately, some marriages move quickly from fantasy to reality to nightmare. What was once a dream-like euphoria over just sitting next to a person soon becomes a detestable state where husband, wife, or both are searching for something else to do. What changes our stories so quickly? What makes marriages so difficult?

First, marriage is difficult because we are human. We continue to play out the story of Adam and Eve. Young love followed by mistakes followed by hiding and then blaming can turn the love you once had into deep reproach. Eve gave into her temptation and Adam followed. Neither said, "no." They were human, full of faults just like we are. Galatians 5:19-21 describes many human characteristics rooted in selfish pride that can destroy a marriage. Idolatry, divisions, strife, jealousy, outbursts of anger, disputes, disagreements, enviousness, and drunkenness are but a few the passage names. Can you pick these out in your marriage?

Instead of being a place of love, some marriages are known for their turmoil. We forgot about what we said on our wedding day & about 1 Corinthians 13, and its description of love. Love is patient, kind, and is not jealous. How many of our marriages can say this? If we were just a little nicer to one another, the home would be much more pleasant. Love does not brag and is not arrogant, does not act unbecomingly; it does not seek its own. Love is not provoked. How often are we ready to defend ourselves when the least little thing is discussed at the dinner table? Love does not take into account a wrong suffered. Are you still bringing up last Christmas? Get over it already. Love does not rejoice in unrighteousness. Love bears all things, believes all things, hopes all things, and endures all things. While our humanity might be our downfall sometimes, it is because of our humanity that we need one another in marriage because love never fails.

John and Stasi Eldredge in their book, *Love and War* say that marriage is also hard because we are both spiritual messes. Marriage exposes our imperfections and incongruities that are somehow supposed to come together. We can either cling to each other for survival, or (as is often the case) kill one another in the process. Through marriage we see each other for who we really are. Men are no longer hopeless romantics and women do take off their make-up. You may find yourself asking your spouse, "Why are you so defensive? Why don't you enjoy going out anymore? Why are you so clingy? I never knew you were an addict." These new realizations cause us to withdraw from the person we have committed to. But we do this forgetting that we ourselves aren't perfect either.

Marriage is symbolic of God's love for us and he uses it to change us. Ephesians 5:31, 32 says, "For this reason a man shall leave his father and mother and shall be joined to his wife, and the two shall become one flesh. This mystery is great; but I am speaking with reference to Christ and the church." Marriage exposes our insecurities and childhood wounds to someone we may not be totally sure we can trust. Just as God sees us for who we are, our spouse soon does the same. God wants to help us heal and through Him we can be whole, especially if we have a loving and understanding spouse by our side.

Jesus said in John 5:39, 40 "You search the Scriptures because you think that in them you have eternal life; it is these that testify about Me; and you are unwilling to come to Me so that you may have life." There's proof all around you that God wants to help. Are you willing? We must rejoin with Christ and His love just as we must rejoin with our spouse. Jesus continues in John 10:10 with, ". . . I came that they may have life, and have it abundantly." This includes your marriage. Imagine. A marriage filled with the abundance of all the things you truly need.

Finally, John and Stasi Eldredge contend that Marriage is hard because it is opposed. It is a central story in the Bible as the good book begins (Genesis 2) and ends (Revelation 21) with a marriage. It is a great love story in the middle of a war. It is a war for our children, our friends, and our souls. Love is the most powerful motivator on Earth and it cannot be found anywhere stronger than in a marriage. Therefore, Satan tries to use it for destruction. Lamentations 1:16 says, "For these things I weep; my eyes run down with water; because far from me is a comforter, One who restores my soul. My children are desolate because the enemy has prevailed." Is he prevailing in your marriage?

All love stories have some sort of conflict and it is this fact that explains why we try to war within the family so much. Satan turns us against one another. He did it in the garden remember? Eve blamed the snake and Adam blamed Eve and then God, "it was the WOMAN that YOU gave me." God uses the family because two are better than one but we mustn't turn on one another. Ecclesiastes 4:9-10 says, "Two are better than one because they have a good return for their labor. For if either of them falls, the one will lift up his companion. But woe to the one who falls when there is not another to lift him up."

The authors go on to say that there are two kinds of people in this world. The first is the clueless. Trust me, you're both difficult to live with. The second type is repentant. They want to do better for their savior and their spouse. I preached this lesson and I wonder how many couples got into their cars with fingers pointed toward the other seat. WRONG! You're both messes, you're both human, and you both need each other. So, quit trying to get him or her to change. Rather, change yourself and pray that God will be a bigger part of your relationship than ever before. This is what you both want; to be full of God's love and then of one another. You can't do this by pointing fingers.

Day 6

Are You Just Married?

The other day my wife saw a bumper sticker that said, "Just Married." She noticed it as being a statement open to interpretation. How did you read it? You probably had one of two reactions. First, maybe you felt good about it. "Ahh, how sweet." Or, you probably said, "yeah, me too" about like you'd say that you were going to get a root canal. If you thought neither, and believe I'm overanalyzing this, let me explain.

In the first case, if you're "Just Married," it's as though you're on a perpetual honeymoon. Your back windshield could still proclaim this feeling of bliss that has been tempered by life yet made better as you have grown closer. The surprises of marriage have actually strengthened your commitment to one another. If you have children, you chose to have them as an expression of your undying love for one another. The commitment you made on your wedding day does not compare with what you feel and believe now because you have seen just how much two people can love one another.

I contend that being "Just Married" in this sense is possible. We eat the same thing over and over again and never tire of it. We go to the same places for vacation and never tire of it. Why can't we be married to the same person and be happy? Bald eagles do it. Why can't we?

The word "Just" in the first scenario describes a point in time while the second use of the word "*just*" minimizes whatever it is describing. "I *just* punched him in the face," your ten year old may say after wrestling with this brother to try and temper your annoyance.

If you're "*just* married" you could also be described as roommates or disgruntled tenants living under the same roof. You're only married on paper and you stay together simply for your children. Stop doing this. Work on your marriage for your children. Soccer can wait. Music lessons can wait. The television can wait. You must connect with your spouse. Otherwise, your family and your friends could potentially experience a trail of pain. If you're *"just* married" your children are learning how not to have an exciting marriage.

By being *"just* married" you rob yourself of the deepest relationship you could have with another human being. He'll make you swoon, and she'll be able to turn the heat up anytime she wants. Do you know how to do these things? If you think this is impossible, then something must change if you're to be truly happy with your spouse. People do it all the time. You JUST have to learn how.

Stop wasting your time by waiting for him to change. It'll never happen. Also, I wouldn't hold my breath on waiting for her to be the wife you've always wanted. You have to work on yourself. Spend time in prayer, and look at what you can do to have the marriage you've always wanted. You might feel like painting "Just Married" on your windshield before you know it.

Day 7

Why Won't My Husband Listen?

In their book, *Distracted: The Erosion of Attention and the Coming Dark Age*, authors Maggie Jackson and Bill McKibben do a wonderful job of explaining how attention works. In marriages, there's a continuing argument that men can only do one thing at a time and women are good multi-taskers. I have heard some women say, "I can watch TV, read a book, vacuum, and cook dinner at the same time all with a baby on my hip." Well, I haven't heard that exact thing but pretty close.

What would Jackson and McKibben say? It is impossible to give our full attention to more than one thing at a time. Can we multi-task? Sure, particularly if it's a simple task, but splitting one's focus between two things demotes both to half a priority each. If a task requires half of your brain and the second tasks requires the other half, then you can't do a third effectively. You can't optimally talk, steer your car, and watch for oncoming traffic at the same time.

What do men like to do? We like to focus and this causes some marital problems. Biologists say that this is brought up from our hunting years when we had to kill our food. Lots of effort and focus is required. Thankfully this is less of a need these days but a skill all the same that can be harnessed.

Men, it's been a joke for centuries that we are tuning our wives out. Some men are because they don't care to hear their wives, but in reality, we are focusing on something else. Use your talent on her and she will appreciate it so much.

By listening to her, you'll show her that you care about her, your relationship, and your family. Being heard is a big emotional need for women and if you meet that, you'll be doing a lot for her relationship by using a talent that you already have. Now that you understand yourself, let's see if we can get her to understand you.

If he's watching the game, get his attention first. Don't expect that he will hear every word you say as soon as you begin to speak. He'll hear something at the second word. He'll realize it's you by the sixth. Then, by the tenth word, he knows he can expect an earful about why he's not listening. He wants to but you can actually be training to not want to. He's focusing, as we've mentioned is an asset, and if you come in to the room talking, he's not going to hear you. This characteristic is what kept birds from distracting us while we were hunting deer to feed our families. You might say that you want to be more important than anything else he is doing. Well, you are. This isn't about that. This is about understanding how your husband focuses. He wants to hear you, but you must let him know you are ready to talk.

Day 8

Give Her What She Needs

In 1982, I was in a theater watching Steven Spielberg's masterpiece, E.T. If you'll remember, E.T. and Elliot were joined through some sort of cosmic bond. Both E.T. and Elliot felt what the other did. At one point, Elliot actually says, "we're fine," alluding to himself and the alien. Elliot even gets physically ill after E.T. is found sick and in a creek bed. Marriage is the same. A spouse's happiness, state of mind, and even emotional health is dependent on the other.

Maybe you have heard some of these aphorisms: "Marriage is a reciprocal relationship where one gives and the other takes and the other gives while the first takes. Marriage is 50/50. Marriage is not always 50/50. Sometimes you have to give more than you receive." There is truth to all of these, but there is a pattern that begins and ends with men. Make your wife happy, she'll make you happy, and you will lack nothing in your relationship.

Men mess up a lot. We are impulsive and loud. We in particular mess up when we only think about what we want which leaves our wives unhappy. We don't look to pleasing our wives because we think we're being pushovers or weak. Plus, we want what we want.

What's interesting is that if this loud, impulsive, self-serving energy can be put in the right direction, we'll be supermen or at least super-husbands. Want a happy marriage? Here's the secret. You must forget about your needs and focus on your wife's. Trust me. When you do this, your needs will be met. A real leader doesn't think of himself, but rather those he is leading. You want to be a leader in your home don't you? Men also want to be taken care of at home, and they want to be admired. Your wife wants to do both of these things. She really does, but you must give her something to love so she'll be motivated to take care of you and admire you.

Well, what does she need? All women want their feelings and point of view to be heard and they want to be loved. Do you know why your wife is upset? Do you know what she means when she says certain things? Women can be difficult to understand but that's because they are so different from men. This does not mean they are impossible to understand. Listen to her and determine what she is trying to tell you. Sometimes it does seem like she's speaking in code, but listen to what she is saying. Communication is a huge need in women. Even if you did the dumbest thing known to man, she will be much quicker to forgive if you show her you understand why she is mad.

The eternal question of, "How do I look" carries a lot with it. Men just want to make sure their fly is up, and if I were to ask my hiking buddies, "How do I look" they'd probably leave me in the woods. For women, the question means a lot more. This question is actually asking, "Do you think I'm beautiful? Do you find me attractive? Would you still come after me if I were not yours?" On this question hangs the balance of mankind. Well, at least your marriage because all women want to be wanted. She takes a long time to get ready. You should notice and learn to really listen because these things mean so much.

Marriage is a functioning machine where two people work to make it happen. Typically, responsibilities are broken up somewhat evenly between the husband and the wife. The wife depends on the husband to do his share, but here's where a bit of difference occurs. The woman depends on you to make her feel loved within her home. How do you do this? You pursue her regularly. She desperately wants this and you desperately want to do it, but maybe you've forgotten. Love and understand her and she'll make sure you are happy.

What happens when you have a happy wife? That wife wants to please her husband. BINGO! Forget about your needs, take care of your wife's, and she will more than take care of yours.

Day 9

Living Your Own Love Story

The romantic genre does not top my list of things to watch and read, but I enjoy spending time with my wife and conversing with her about what she enjoys which often includes the latest Nicholas Sparks phenomenon. Therefore, I've learned a great deal about this multi-million dollar market.

One of the things I know is that women like romance movies and books, and if men can understand why, they can make their spouses' lives best-sellers. The latest chick-flick I saw was "Dear John," and I really enjoyed it. It is what I would call a man-friendly love story since the hero isn't a blubbering Englishman (i.e. Hugh Grant). Channing Tatum plays John Tyree, a special-forces soldier in the Iraq war who can kick some serious butt. You can't get much manlier than that.

According to Catherine Lanigan, author of *Writing the Great American Romance Novel*, all romances are pretty much the same as far as the character elements. In her book, she describes the male hero as someone who is compassionate. He must care about those around him and about what he believes in. Lanigan says that if he's not compassionate, he's just a "cold fish or possibly a psychopath."

Second, the character must be strong in some way. It can be physical prowess, but it can also be commitment to his ideals or in his judgment ability. Next, he must be intelligent and have common sense.

Kindness is an important characteristic of all leading men, but don't mistake kindness for weakness. He's never kind to the villains. The hero must also be loyal to the heroine because he will always choose her over everything else. He's also loyal to those things and people that are important to him. The hero has manners, is complimentary, and never rude except when he has to handle the bad guys.

The final and most important characteristic of a hero in a love story is the fact that he has some sort of flaw. Without this, there is no conflict and subsequently there is no excitement. In "Dear John" Tyree's flaw was his relationship with his father; something many men can relate to. What is your life's conflict or your character flaw? What are you doing about it? The answers to these questions may be exactly what your marriage needs.

The imperfection makes the character real, creating a more compelling story. It's what can make your wife love you too. Sound strange? In romances, it is the hero's love for the female character that spurs his development in overcoming the flaw. He wants to do better because of her. This is a tremendous compliment to womanhood and your wife will melt when she realizes what you're doing.

Jack Nicholson said it best to Helen Hunt in "As Good As It Gets." I refer to this movie often, but it's so true. Nicholson's character has stumbled through the entire movie trying to win Hunt's heart. On the surface he's somewhat of a non-hero but look closely, and you'll see that he has all the ingredients I've mentioned here. It's just that his flaw, Obsessive Compulsive Disorder, is so pronounced. As the movie climaxes, she begs him to make their dinner date memorable. Like many women, she longs for a romantic moment. He nervously fumbles with his words and finally says to her, "You make me want to be a better man." Shocked, Hunt's character replies, "That's maybe the best compliment of my life." All the terrible things he had done were gone as she finally saw her crucial place in his life. Hunt begins to like him because it was evident that he was willing to change, learn, and be better than he was all for her. Are you willing to do the same for your spouse?

In short, be a good man to those around you and work to become the man your wife will be proud of and want to be with.

Day 10

The Women In Love Stories

What can women learn from the main female characters in romance novels? In her book, *Writing the Great American Romance Novel*, Catherine Lanigan discusses several characteristics that are imperative for the female heroine to have in any romance story. I believe these are also characteristics that are important to a husband and to a woman's children as they look to her to be all that she can be for them and for herself.

Just like the male character, the female has an obstacle that she must overcome. This spurs the excitement in the story. In all romance novels, the female star is the "cog of the wheel" and everything else revolves around her. Sounds pretty good doesn't it? In a well-written romance novel, the character works through the chaos of the story using her strengths.

The female character must be intelligent. This is a similar characteristic to her male counterpart. Something that must take place with her however is that she must listen to those wise friends around her as she evolves into a better person. Both the male and female characters grow in the story.

Different from her male counterpart, the female must listen to her intuition. This is a big strength with women in general. Men have an inkling of it too; it's just that they don't listen to it very much. We're too analytical sometimes. Inherent in the story format is that the woman must listen to her heart and be open to love.

She must be compassionate in an active way. She roots for the underdog, stands in picket lines and speaks her mind. She is the kind of nurturing friend that all females hope to be. She is courageous and in romance novels, she finally discovers the courage to love. This is part of the conflict. After being hurt or pursuing a career for far too long, the crisis in the story must push the female towards the ability to love. As the story climaxes, she realizes that she can't live her life or fight her battles alone. This is the driving force that pushes her towards the hero, which is what the romance is about, and should be what your marriage is about.

Your kids, your career, and your parents are all important but none of them can carry you off into the sunset the way your man can. All men want a beauty by their side and Lanigan discusses the importance of the beauty characteristic. As we know, beauty must be internal and external.

What causes some women to lose their inner beauty? Some women grow bitter for a variety of reasons. They were hurt by their father and therefore are unable to make a deep connection with a man. They don't like themselves and can't see why anyone would love them. These are personal matters that if explored and resolved can increase the beauty in a woman tenfold.

Those women you admire in romance novels so much, what about them do you appreciate and how can you be like them? Their example can be a chance for incredible growth in your life. Trust me, your husband and children will love you for it.

Day 11

Scrooge On Marriage

In the movie, "A Christmas Carol" there is a very good scene where Ebenezer is conversing with his fiancé, Belle. She is obviously distraught, because of pleading with him to love her and of the recent deaths of her parents. He had committed to her through a "contract" but it was clear to Belle that he loved money more than he did her. Scrooge is cold towards Belle as you realize that this is in the early days of his business. They bicker back and forth about money. His pursuit of wealth had grown immense. Then she asks him a very important question. It's the question women ask of their husbands every day. ". . . if you were free today, tomorrow, yesterday, would you choose me -- you who make your every decision by how much profit it will bring. If you could forget about money for a time and choose me, would you regret your choice?"

Every woman asks this of her husband either verbally or with her actions. When she dresses nice she wants to be noticed. When you see one another after work, the clock is ticking until you acknowledge her with a kiss and she notices if you take a long time. Every so often she wants to hear why you chose her and whether or not you'd do it again. These moments can sweep her off her feet. So, why not do it? Are you scared? Men must be purposeful in everything, but especially in things that pertain to the care of their wives. It won't just happen. You have to make it happen.

Too many men choose other things. Some, like Scrooge, do so because they give their heart to something else. They find pleasure in an activity or other woman and thus neglect the one they pledged their love to. Some choose other things because the level of commitment needed to make a marriage thrive is often difficult to maintain. If you've seen "Ghosts of Girlfriends Past" (a Scrooge parody) you'll know that Matthew Mcconaughey's character is afraid of being with one woman. He's AFRAID. Men like this won't admit it, but going from relationship to relationship is easier than trying to make one woman happy. Doing this may be tough, but it's one of the most fulfilling things that can be done.

Finally, men neglect their wives in the name of taking care of them. "If I work harder, my wife will have more things, and she'll be happier." All the money in the world can't buy happiness. Scrooge found this out, but today some of us can't see it. There is fulfillment that can be found in a well paying job, but what really matters is how we spend our free time with those we love. You can't hug clothing or have dinner with a diamond necklace. Men, for your wife and children your time is the best thing you can give them. Christmas morning presents are exciting but the most important gifts can't be wrapped.

Day 12

Are You A Marital Humbug?

After Scrooge's visit with his various ghosts, he chooses to be a peaceful man who loves all he sees. Unfortunately, it took him seeing his own tombstone and the wretched life he lived to make this move. It seems in marriages that some husbands and wives are just as miserable as Ebenezer. There's very little joy and each breath that is taken robs another second of what could be a joyous life. When there's not something deeper at play, all many couples may need to do is choose. Will it be misery or will it be peace?

When you choose to notice everything he/she does wrong, you are choosing misery. If you live with someone long enough, you are going to find plenty wrong with him or her. This is often a distraction in order to avoid your own misgivings but there you are, noticing all the inconsistencies of your spouse and wondering why you ever got married. Scrooge saw all that was wrong with those who walked through his door. If you search for bad, you'll find it. Looking for good can make for a much happier home.

When you choose to argue rather than love, you are choosing misery. There's something about being at war with your spouse. Some seem to enjoy it. We are not happy and he/she is supposed to make us happy. I'M NOT HAPPY SO IT MUST BE YOUR FAULT! You're probably not happy because you're finding all of your spouse's faults and not working on your own. If you are one half of a whole that is supposed to be about love, what are you bringing to the table?

You choose misery when you only think of yourself. What can please me! This will lead to an unfulfilling life as it did for Scrooge. He only thought of himself but when he began to look of the welfare of others, he found joy. Being in a relationship with another human being can be so rewarding. However, if you don't think of that other person, there will be no joy.

Finally, you choose misery when you refuse to meet your spouse's needs. Much of the arguing in a marriage comes from not meeting one another's needs. It's strange however because this is really why we got married in the first place; that person met a need of ours. Are you refusing to talk to her? Have you decided to not like what he enjoys? There will be war.

You choose peace when you decide (or re-decide) to make a life with that person. You choose peace when you offer forgiveness and a total acceptance of that other person despite their faults. You choose peace when you find some way to enjoy the time of being together rather than despising it. When you choose peace, you choose your words carefully, your actions carefully, and your thoughts carefully in order to make a life that is less like that of Ebenezer Scrooge and more like a family you can be proud of.

Day 13

How Dependable Is Your Memory?

I have an ongoing feud with some of my coworkers. Here's my dilemma. In the 1990's Life cereal commercial, do the boys give Mikey the cereal because he likes or dislikes everything? I have heard jokes repeatedly based on Mikey LIKING everything. "Let Jim try it, he'll eat anything." They usually say this in reference to me. I think it has something to do with me drinking hot wing sauce once, but I don't know.

I once thought Mikey liked everything, but knew this didn't make advertising sense. What would the value of the cereal be if the boy liked everything? When I told others of my observation I was quickly reprimanded and informed of my ignorance. Well, through an extensive YouTube search I discovered that they had Mikey try the cereal because he DIDN'T like to eat certain things. Look it up!

I say this in jest, but also to prove a point; memory is extremely faulty and unreliable. Laurence Gonzales in his book, *Deep Survival*, quotes a study by neuroscientist Joseph LeDoux. In it, LeDoux concludes that the part of our brain that recalls information is not the same part of our brain that formed the initial memory. In other words, we store a memory with one portion of our brain, but recall it with another. His point is that we sometimes kill ourselves accidentally because of bad decisions based on recalled memory.

Do you ever have an argument with your spouse about the scotch tape and its last location? "I know I put it there! It's got to be here!!" Then, when your spouse finds it elsewhere, your memory is revived. Ooops. You're angry or your loved one is angry because of your out of control rage that seizes you when the scotch tape should be in the drawer next to the dishwasher. Maybe that's just me.

Arguments spun from "I know I put it there" or "I'm sure of it" aren't worth arguing about. It has been my experience as a recaller of information that it's better to err on the side of being wrong and being proven right than being right and then being proven wrong. Remember, if you can, that our memories are pretty undependable.

Day 14

Fighting to Stay Together

Through my private counseling practice, I see two kinds of couples. The first comes in the office fighting and, in early sessions, leaves fighting. The second type is quiet and at least one spouse will say very little. This couple is often the most difficult to work with.

If there is no other explanation, this quiet characteristic usually means that the spouse had given up. He or she no longer cares about the marriage and thus is not willing to contribute to the sessions. In order to convince their partner that they had "tried everything," he or she was simply attending so the divorce papers could be signed.

It worries me more when apathy, rather than arguing, is the tension in a marriage. Apathy, or a lack of caring, indicates someone has given up. When someone has given up, they don't see the point in trying anymore. No more fighting. So, I like working with the couple that yells and argues a lot; even when it's at me.

In many cases, couples who argue really want their marriage to work. One young couple I saw wouldn't even sit beside each other at our first session. They screamed and seemed to have a general distaste for one another. It wasn't easy, but after they saw the value in doing things differently, they were even more willing to commit to change. They slowly became a constructive husband and wife rather than an at-war couple. They learned how to enjoy one another again.

This idea may seem strange, but do you know how exhausting arguing is? Tension at home that funnels into work, and you generally spend all your time thinking about your spouse. Why would anyone put so much energy into something they didn't care about? When these types of feelings are present, the couple still cares, they are just putting their energy into all the wrong things; things that sabotage the marriage rather than build it up.

Willard F. Harley, Jr. in his book, *Fall In Love, Stay In Love*, discusses the concept of the love bank. Everything you do as a spouse either makes a deposit or a withdrawal from your spouse's love bank.

When a deposit is made, your spouse feels loved, but when a withdrawal is made, a negative feeling takes over. Now, we are all going to make mistakes from time to time, but the goal is to make more deposits than withdrawals. We make deposits when we kiss, hug, and consider one another's feelings.

Too many spouses skip out on affection and neglect their spouse in their daily activities even though the preacher pronounced them as "one." While a spouse may feel justified in making a major purchase without discussing it or coming in late without calling; if it hurts the one they are supposed to love and cherish it is a withdrawal. These actions, which may seem harmless on the surface, may only get you deeper into withdrawals because you are not considering the other party. Why wouldn't this be harmful?

What are you doing that hurts your marriage? What can you do to make it better? If you want a happy home, you must answer these questions. This way you are forced to think about your actions, doing those things that ensure your marriage's success rather than its volatility.

Day 15

Looking for Greener Grass?

Family Feud; what a great show. I watched it when I was a child and I catch it from time to time even now. My Sunday school teacher was actually on an episode once. If you pay attention, you can occasionally get a glimpse into societal trends; well, at least trends among 100 people. A few weeks ago one of the questions was, "On a scale from one to ten (ten being the best) how happy is your marriage?" The number one answer? One.

Through Facebook I have discovered that some of my friends from high school are divorced and I'm only 34. Not what I would wish upon anyone. There are many answers to marital difficulties and some turn to divorce. I wonder though if people turn to divorce too quickly sometimes. Now, I don't want any part in dealing out guilt for past divorces. I am much more content being about the business of helping people deal with their current situations and their future. So, stopping divorces and improving current marriages (be they second or third) is more my game.

Greater than 50% of marriages end in divorce and a majority of those remarry. Statistics show that with each marriage, the percentage of divorce continues to rise. I'm not sure why this is not mentioned very often. I think it might actually make people reconsider their decision to separate causing them to work harder at making their current marriages work; saving a lot of heartache.

One explanation for this pattern of increasing divorce in subsequent marriages is that marital difficulties are often recreated when the issues that brought a couple to divorce are not dealt with. Different couple, same problems. If one spouse has a particular personality difficulty or marriage-ending habit, he or she may carry that into the next marriage unless major changes occur.

While dating we spend so much time making sure the other person is happy with us. However, as the years pass for a husband and wife the fire does seem to go out and one or both spouses start looking elsewhere for a match.

When you act like you're in love with someone who is lovable (a key component indeed), the feeling will often follow. If not, there may be something else going on. If you remarry and neglect correcting your mistakes, don't expect things to be different. The unfulfilling pattern in your most important relationship this side of eternity continues.

A former professor of mine, the late Bill Greenwalt, often said this in regards to those who remarry. "The grass might be greener, but you still have to mow it." Marriages have to be worked on, love has to be cultivated, and if these things do not happen in the first marriage, the chances may be slim that they will happen in the second.

Day 16

How To Get Out of the Dog House

Sometimes men don't think before they speak and they end up hurting their wives' feelings. Men want to take care of their wives so it should upset them when they hurt the one they are supposed to protect. However, it can be frustrating, as men don't always understand what is going on in their wives' heads. Also, simple apologies will not always work especially when you really mess up. There has to be more involved. Well, I hope this can shed some light on the subject for when you stick your foot in your mouth. Trust me. It's going to happen.

An understanding of your wife's mentality during these times is important. First, when you say something upsetting to your wife, she might not let you know right away. This happens because she wants you to realize what you've done on your own. She's actually giving you a chance to redeem yourself. She doesn't want to have to tell you. So, if things are going well when you first get home but they suddenly change, you need to think back and analyze the evening. What could you have said or done that was upsetting to her? Then, go give her a hug, and very specifically confess your wrong. Don't beat around the bush but be sincere. It goes a long way. She might not perk up immediately, but your gesture will help get that process started. She'll feel better soon enough and she'll know you care.

Second, when you say something stupid, sometimes you know it. As the words leave your mouth, you can't stop them. The guy who keeps your mouth in check is on a coffee break or something. Then, just as the last word exits your melon, you look at your lovely wife and for some reason the phrase, "a woman scorned" comes to mind. Give her time to be upset and offer a heartfelt apology when appropriate. See my first suggestion and remember that flowers the next day or a meal out that evening can really help.

Let's say you've racked your brain over the evening and you

can't think of anything that you've done. You know she spoke to someone on the phone, but you don't know what about. There's your first clue. Also, you don't know how her day has gone because you've not had a chance to ask her yet. Here's the good news. It might not be about you. Maybe you did say or do something silly. This may have upset her, but had an earlier event not taken place, she wouldn't be this way. Your normal action was just the catalyst that brought out her emotions. When you realize it's not you, don't act like, "Wow! I'm glad it's not me." They'll know what you're thinking and any sincerity you try to dish out here won't matter.

What should you always keep in mind? When you've done something wrong, she wants you to know it. She wants you to be remorseful and simply saying you're sorry won't cut it. Unless her feelings are understood, she won't be satisfied. This isn't a revenge kind of thing. It's more about empathy. She wants to hear that you know why what you did was hurtful to her. Women love being understood. How would you feel if she said or did the same thing to you? "It wouldn't bother me," is not the correct answer. Put yourself in her shoes. Imagine how you'd feel if the tables were turned.

This is just one facet of understanding that I hope I can give you as you work to be the best husband you can for the one who gives you her all.

Day 17

Stop Doing the Wrong Things

A couple falls in love, marries, and then they seem to grow apart. What causes this? I believe it can be traced to two things: our concept of love and our concept of what we expect to feel in a marriage.

In regards to the first, some cultures get married and then fall in love. In America, we fall in love and get married. Although, I don't believe it's actual "love" since a level of commitment is involved which takes time to prove and experience. We expect marital bliss to continue for years with little effort on our part. That's basically how we got started; we saw the person and we melted. Well, bitterness sets in as we see all the things that are wrong with the person. This is a formula for disaster. Unlike when we were young or dating in college, work takes up a great deal of our time and then children come into the picture and (let's be honest) suck the life out of us. What should you do to save your failing marriage? Start doing the right things and stop doing the wrong.

In *Fighting for Your Marriage*, authors Markman, Stanley, and Blumberg say to avoid the following:

Escalation – "Escalation occurs when partners respond back and forth negatively to each other, continually upping the ante so the conversation gets more and more hostile." 1 Peter 3:9 says, "Do not repay evil with evil or insult with insult." Don't cause the argument to get worse. Be level headed, particularly if your partner isn't. Peace was never found between two people if they both want war.

Negative Interpretation – "Negative interpretations occur when one partner consistently believes that the motives of the other are more negative than is really the case." Just because your partner says something does not mean that it is meant as a derogatory comment. Work on communication means you must put your guards down. Discuss it if your partner's comments hurt, but don't assume anything.

Invalidation – Listen to the other person's feelings and validate them. By name calling and disregarding what the other person is saying or feeling, you are building a wall of division rather than trust or love. Hear his/her feelings or thoughts and let them know you understand then work to be understood yourself.

Withdrawal – With these first three in place, emotional and even physical withdrawal is sure to follow. We avoid people that are not pleasing to be around. Stop doing these wrong things and reconnect.

Day 18

Failing Restaurants / Failing Marriages

One of my favorite shows is Ramsay's Kitchen Nightmares. The famed French chef, Gordon Ramsay, goes to failing restaurants and, after digging through the rancid meat in their coolers, turns the pub, cafe, or family eatery into a must-visit location.

Typically the owners of the restaurant are hanging on by a thread. They seem to be doing all the wrong things and it soon becomes obvious as to why the place is failing. Owners who don't need to be in the kitchen and cooks who have no sense of taste are driving the restaurant into the ground.

An episode I saw today showed the owner trying out some of the new food by Ramsay, simple and tasty. His own menu just wasn't working. How can a cook, or anyone in the restaurant business, not be able to tell if something is good? They get distracted and forget why they got into the industry in the first place. This is kind of like a husband or wife not being good at their respective roles in the home. You dated all that time and were so good at it. What has happened? You have forgotten to put effort into your relationship. It's as simple as doing the following things:

Speak kindly to one another.

Send flowers, just because.

Or buy a gift, just because.

Pour his/her coffee in the morning.

Talk

Do things together

Care

Discuss what you like and dislike

By not doing good things, you'll begin to do bad things and this is a very slow process that can destroy your marriage. Make a conscious effort. You feel good when you give and good when you get. If it's a priority, you both will be blessed.

Day 19

Do Affairs Just Happen?

Extramarital affairs are devastating to everyone. The betrayed spouse, kids, immediate family, and even friends and coworkers bear the brunt of this earth-shattering event.

After the infidelity is discovered, the unfaithful often say, "We never intended for this to happen." True. Most spouses don't set out, when leaving for work, to come home having begun an inappropriate relationship. However, things like this don't "just happen." Many factors contribute.

There's a commercial on television for the Plan B pill (which I do not endorse). It is a contraception that stops a pregnancy before it begins. Their slogan is, "Because the unexpected happens." I'm sure the unexpected does, but I can't help but think when I see this TV spot, "If you have unprotected sex, you could get pregnant. What did you think would happen? Were you sleeping in health class?" The same is true with affairs. While someone may never set out to have an affair, if you neglect your spouse and develop an attraction to someone else, what do you think is going to happen?

Another response is, "It just happened." This statement, as well as the first, minimizes the events leading to the affair and also the hurtful ripple affect that will be felt for years. It's like saying that September 11, "just happened." Both statements give little credence to what has occurred and, for this reason, both are quite maddening to the betrayed.

Many marriages end when an affair takes place, but if you decide to work things out, there are some things that must occur. The cheater must grasp the extent of his or her behavior, and this understanding must be communicated to the hurting spouse. An empathic understanding is key. In regards to the offended spouse, his/her part in this must be seen as well. Maybe he or she spent too much time doing something else. Oftentimes an affair can be the result of what both spouses have or have not done.

If you decide to work things out, keep in mind that it is a great deal of work. I have a slogan on my office wall that says, "Every true strength is gained through struggle." You are in a relationship that must be maintained and through better or worse, you can have a stronger marriage.

Day 20

Find Him to Find Her

"A woman's heart should be so lost in God that a man must seek Him to find her."

This has been attributed to a woman by the name of Elisabeth Elliot and even Maya Angelou. Either way, I believe it sums up a great deal about marriage. If a man and woman are to have the ultimate joy in their life of being with one another, they must have a relationship with Christ.

Much about your relationship together is dictated by what you do apart from one another and with God. Paul says it well in I Corinthians 7:1-6 says, *"Now concerning the things whereof ye wrote unto me: It is good for a man not to touch a woman. Nevertheless, to avoid fornication, let every man have his own wife, and let every woman have her own husband. Let the husband render unto the wife due benevolence: and likewise also the wife unto the husband. The wife hath not power of her own body, but the husband: and likewise also the husband hath not power of his own body, but the wife. Defraud ye not one the other, except it be with consent for a time, that ye may give yourselves to fasting and prayer; and come together again, that Satan tempt you not for your incontinency. But I speak this by permission, and not of commandment."*

Why else should a man and woman seek to be close to God for each other?

Only by experiencing the level of forgiveness God offers will you be able to extend any forgiveness in your own marriage.

Only by learning about the love that God has for you will you be able to extend that love to another person.

Only if you are humbled as Jesus instructs will you look to meet the needs of your spouse before your own.

Day 21

How to Be Romantic

Some men are natural romantics and others couldn't get a girl's attention at a kissing booth for charity. Maybe being a romantic is a skill and maybe it isn't. Either way, it can be learned.

First, learn about the restaurants in your area. Right now I can tell you which restaurants have private tables, which deliver flowers upon your arrival, and which you should avoid. Inherent in being a romantic is the characteristic of forethought. You thought about the restaurant, you bought the card, and you surprised her with a gift she wasn't expecting.

Second, mark important days in a calendar. Even if you don't have a schedule for anything else, you must mark things to remember for your wife. If you're stopping at Walgreens on February 14 to buy a bear holding a heart, and you're not a ten-year-old, don't bother going home.

Third, learn your wife's gift needs. Sometimes men approach the gift question based on what they want to do. So ask yourself, "what does my wife enjoy." Unless she has a curio cabinet with missing pieces to her fairy collection, you need to really listen to her when she says she likes something. Make a mental note and return to buy it. Also, talk to her about flowers and gifts. She may rather have an evening without the kids than a dozen roses that won't last a week.

Finally, listen to her. Most all women like to talk and all women love being understood. If talking isn't your favorite thing to do, make it your goal that evening to really listen to her. It's your task. Ask questions if you don't understand and repeat what she said back to her to show her you are listening.

Romance is the spice in your marriage. Think it's just about her? It isn't. It's as much about you. Romance is what can make you come alive again as a man because you are winning the attention of a woman; YOUR woman. Make it happen tonight.

Day 22

Why You Shouldn't Get Angry

What causes an argument between a husband and a wife? Two people are mad at each other. What can stop an argument between a husband and a wife? Somebody not getting mad and thinking with a level head. The goal is to get both to do this, but one step at a time.

The wife becomes upset at something, addresses it with the husband in a very offensive manner. Does she need to temper this? Sure. But the husband can do his part early on by deciding to not get upset as well. Self-control is an admirable trait.

There are two reasons the husband (or wife if the circumstances are reversed) shouldn't get mad. First, if he's done something wrong, he can apologize and by admitting fault in a humble way, the wife will really appreciate him. At least she will when she's calmed down. It takes a big man to admit his mistakes and then to learn from them. The second reason a husband shouldn't get mad is because if he hasn't done something wrong and the wife is ugly about it, her apology will be that much sweeter. Be sure not to rub it in her face, though.

We all want peace in our homes and both parties have to work for it. Here are some tips on how to do this. The following methods can almost guarantee peace in your home.

Don't get mad at anything. This may seem impossible, but what good does it do? Getting mad won't get the floor swept or materialize the forks that were forgotten on the picnic. Anger is typically a sign that effective communication isn't occurring. We're mad because we don't believe we're being heard. Talk about it. Don't yell about it.

Don't be accusatory. Is he really trying to make your life miserable or is he just forgetful. If you accuse him of something, he will get defensive.

Work to please your spouse. If you want to be happy, make someone else happy and he or she will do the same for you. Work to remember important dates and always meet his or her needs. Love in a home takes effort.

Don't get defensive. The issue isn't about you. It's about your family's well being. If you're constantly messing up, work to stop and become a better husband, wife, mother, or father. Then, your family will flourish.

Day 23

Stop Agreeing & Start Building

In their book, *Love & War: Finding the Marriage You've Dreamed Of*, John & Stasi Eldredge do a magnificent job of laying out the spiritual connections of marriage. In chapter six they discuss agreements we make with ourselves and how this is nothing but the work of Satan wanting to destroy our marriages. He is the father of lies and we often believe them. With these agreements in place, your marriage will never be what it truly can and should be.

These agreements are attempts at maintaining our marital relationship in its current state with no desire to improve. If any of these sentiments remain unchecked, divorce can be close, and if not divorce, an unsatisfying relationship will continue. Satan came in between one of the world's most famous couples, Adam and Eve. They blamed one another for their situation at the tree when Satan lied to them.

Some examples of these agreements are:

It's just not going to get any better.

Don't rock the boat; settle for what you've got.

It's not worth the effort; don't give it one more try.

Never let anyone hurt you again.

I'm just not going to trust her/him anymore.

You do your thing and I'll do mine.

I shouldn't have married him/her.

I'd be happier with someone else.

If you watch political shows, you'll notice that whoever is speaking will put their own "spin" on the situation. Conservatives say that Obama is spending us into oblivion while more liberal shows would say that Obama is changing us for the better. Whichever way you lean will determine whom you believe. The same can happen in your marriage when a simple event turns into a reason to be upset with your spouse.

You're in a hurry and she wants to talk about something important. "Why does she always do this?" is what you say to yourself as you rush out the door. Then on your way to work, the irritation festers, and in a sick way, you enjoy it. Sort of like picking a scab. You know it's bad but you do it anyway. You think to yourself, "I hate it when she does that. She's such a nag. It will never change." Eldredge and Eldredge say, "Irritation becomes cynicism; cynicism becomes resignation." Turning a simple conversation into something darker damages your marriage all because you agree to do so.

Whatever happened to considering our spouse's heart and his or her needs? Instead of moments of connection, important moments turn into mine fields; reason to feel contempt rather than love. We must stop making these negative agreements and start considering those things that strengthen our marriage. If you are in a negative pattern, get out of it and work to build your bond rather than agreeing with yourself to tear it down.

Day 24

Black Widow Syndrome

Have you ever been sitting with a group of friends and one of the husbands in the group makes a comment about something he has done or would like to do? You listen attentively and the next sound you hear is the sarcastic laughter of his wife followed by a verbal assault on how he never would or could do that. OUCH! I hate those moments. What behavior from a man could warrant such demeaning words from someone who should love him? However, I also think, "What is he doing or not doing at home?" Is he just putting on a show for us, and she is tired of hearing it?

In either case, my answer to the men is this. Don't give her a reason to make you a laughing stock in front of your friends. Does she respect you? If not, there may be a good reason. Almost every little girl wants her Prince Charming and once she's grown up; her vision of him has not changed much. She wants a strong leader for her home who can make confident decisions while still encouraging her to grow in her potential as a woman.

Does she nag? She may not want to do this but maybe it's the only thing that can get you motivated. Nagging becomes a pattern typically because asking wasn't getting the job done. First, she asks you to do something. Second, you don't do it and this pattern continues until the "Honey dears" become "GET OFF THE COUCH AND FIX THE TOILET!" The more this is done, the more she expects that she will have to irritate you to death in the future to get anything accomplished. You're not taking care of business, so she has to in her own way. What's worse, there may be more important things than honey-dos that she's missing from you.

As you know, the female Black Widow kills the male after they mate. Apparently, she learned early on that he was not going to take care of business so she had to. See the link? I wish our homes did not resemble this, but sadly, many do. The man does his thing, the woman does hers and the only thing missing when an argument erupts is a little venom and a red hour glass.

To the women I would say, "Is your laughter warranted?" Nothing can reduce your man to a mouse quicker than parading his failures around for everyone to see. While he should work every day at being a stronger man for his family, making him the butt of jokes (which for some reason is politically correct) will not help him in this journey. It will only make the obstacles seem more insurmountable as he works to thwart off your attacks too.

Secondly, is your nagging warranted? Too often we focus on what is not being done. Have you noticed what is being done? What is he good at? Asking this question will help you see the good in him as you help him be a better man. He wants to be your prince. Help him with this by not making him an ogre.

Once a balance is reached, the husband and wife learn they can depend on one another and are better for it.

Day 25

Get Marriage Counselling or A Helmet

In August of 1993, I was playing football for Smith County High School (Carthage, TN). At the opening jamboree, we played Trousdale County High School (TCHS). It did not go well because TCHS kept in their best players the entire time when it's customary to play most of your squad. As we were leaving the field after the game, a fight broke out. I was in the middle of the crowd and when I looked behind me, players were taking off their helmets and racing to the action in order to join in the melee. It's funny because this was the original reason our schools hadn't played each other in years.

When a crowd is doing something, the individuals within that crowd are likely to follow suit whether they know what is happening or not. Thousands of people are running to something at a concert? No thought is given to what it might be, more people join in and many are trampled and possibly even killed. In Tom Cruise's version of "War of the Worlds," droves of people are running to get out of the city. This made them an easier target for the aliens. Not until Cruise took his own path did he find safety. A reaction to the emotional atmosphere around us is typical, but in the real and fictitious examples above, we can be lead to our demise if we don't think.

This happens in our marriages too because much emotion can be found here. Your spouse is upset, says something to you and then you become upset. A verbal fight breaks out and you take your helmet off when helmets are going to be flying. Not too smart. What did I do that hot day in 1993? I put my helmet on and backed up to see what I needed to do. I pulled one of our guys off of theirs and it was over as quickly as it had begun. In your marriage, if the dam of emotion breaks, you both can be swept away and injury can occur.

If you are fighting, the problem quite possibly began long before the first word was spoken out of anger. This is known as chaos theory or "the butterfly effect." Small differences in initial conditions will result in outcomes that are opposing. In other words, the fight actually began long before one of our hot-headed assistant coaches traded words with one of theirs. It began when their first string played our second or maybe even years before with bad blood between our towns. Similarly, arguments with your spouse or your children begin long before the first word is exchanged.

Here are some things to consider if you believe you are about to go down the rapids of an argument. How are you feeling? Are you irritated? What about? Is it something your spouse did? Is it worth discussing or are you the one with the problem? Should you just forget it? If it is with your spouse, and he/she begins asking you questions that aren't helping the situation, tell him you need some time alone and that you can come back later to discuss it.

Let's say you are attacked out of nowhere. Back up and ask, "What is happening?" "What can I do?" With this mentality, a solution can quickly be found. Here are some steps to consider if this is the case: First, think back to when you might have hurt his/her feelings or said something inappropriate. The quicker you can communicate this to your spouse, the better he/she will be relieved that you understand. Second, listen and try not to become defensive. Your goal here is to resolve the issue, not to be sleeping on the couch that night. Keep this in mind and your pride will be retained as you make a huge decision to listen, grow and meet your spouse's needs.

Day 26

You Can Have A Royal Marriage

While I didn't wake up at 3AM CST to watch the wedding of the year, (Kate & William) I did watch it at 5:30AM and I'm glad I did. The Right Reverend and Right Honourable Dr. Richard Chartres' remarks about marriage were so inspiring.

"Marriage is intended to be a way in which man and woman help each other to become what God meant each one to be, their deepest and truest selves."

While these are beautiful words, they are also dreadfully difficult to bear and enact in our own lives. Our true selves are often scary and many of us do not want to expose our inner demons to someone else. This is where lots of marital conflicts arise; we feel vulnerable and we don't like it so we become defensive.

However, as with Christ's forgiveness and total acceptance, a loving spouse will see past our weaknesses and love us unconditionally too. Why can't you get along with your spouse? It may be because your relationship with Christ is weak or even non-existent. A man can't know what Ephesians 5:25 means when it says, "Husbands, love your wives, just as Christ also loved the church and gave Himself up for her . . ." if Christ is not in his life.

Chartres observed that we cannot have a full relationship with our spouse because we have allowed "the reality of God to fade" from our lives. We expect our spouse to fulfill our every need and this is unfair to our spouses. Some of our needs go beyond what any human can meet because we are terrestrial and spiritual beings.

Dr. Chartres went on to say, "the more we give of self, the richer we become in soul;" This too is difficult to understand, but as Christ washed the disciples' feet, He experienced the blessing of humility. As we look past our own needs to meet that of our spouse's, we will become rich with the blessings this offers.

Many are reluctant to give of themselves because they have been hurt somehow. Whether through a family member, an ex-spouse, or even the current one, pain can flow into all parts of our life. This can keep us from truly living with ourselves and then openly with someone else. If we accept God's forgiveness, we can have it in our marriages too.

I love it when Chartres said, "It is possible to transform [our spouse] as long as we do not harbor ambitions to reform our partner." If we love our spouse, we will help them become who they can be and if he/she is willing, they will grow along with us.

It's never too late for a relationship with Christ or with one's spouse because as Chartres said, "In marriage we are seeking to bring one another into fuller life." While we admire Kate & William, Chartres said that "In a sense every wedding is a royal wedding . . . making a new life together so that life can flow through them into the future." Is your marriage suffering? You're never too far-gone in a marriage to save it so long as you're willing to make the trip back.

Day 27

Gift Giving 101 for Husbands

When the Christmas season ends, another gift-giving time approaches that carries more importance than ten Christmases; Valentines Day. Husbands, maybe you messed up on December 25, when she opened "his and hers" fly rods, but as February 14, approaches, you have a marvelous chance to redeem yourselves.

I hope that my tips here help you better than Neil Cavuto's advice to buy her a cheese and pepperoni tray from a mall kiosk. This is your wife, not your great aunt. To be fair, his advice was about surviving the holiday rush. Over the next week though you can certainly find your wife something meaningful. The only rush you have to worry about here is the one you may find yourself in at Wal-Mart on February 13th. Prepare and you will succeed.

First, be careful of the chocolate myth. Pepe Le Peu did it all the time but that doesn't mean you should. If a woman is self-conscious about her body then all she will see inside that heart shaped box is something else that makes her feel bad. The same thing goes with clothes. Unless she has tried on the outfit and just not bought it yet, clothing is a bad idea. Just because it's her size, it doesn't mean she'll like how it looks.

"What would she like?" This is the wrong question that too many men ask because it can be answered this way, "She would love tickets to a mixed martial arts competition . . . if she liked that kind of thing." The "if" part is what many men miss because "would" gets in the way and absolutely directs you to no details. You need to ask, "What DOES she like" and go from there.

Ask her what she wants but if she says, "it doesn't matter" or anything else that leaves it up to you be careful. Exercise equipment, cooking utensils or a new vacuum are gambles. Maybe she's mentioned it and you think it would be OK . . . stop right there. The fact is, when she leaves it up to you, she wants to be surprised and she wants you to be romantic.

To surprise her, ask yourself the following. "If she had five hours by herself, what would she do?" "If money wasn't an issue, what would she want?" This is Valentine's Day, you're supposed to spend a little. "What is her favorite restaurant and how can I make the experience even better?"

I prefer local jewelers to the large chain stores. You don't have to be an expert to get her anything good. First, you can get her something to match what she already has. If she has diamond earrings, a diamond necklace isn't hard to find. Another advantage to going local is that when the jeweler is the owner, he'll treat you right. He doesn't need a sale, he needs your business and he'll go the extra mile to make you happy. You can't put a price on that. Maybe it doesn't look like they have a lot in the case, but they have tons of catalogs behind the counter and can put something together for you. This will really impress her and it won't cost you any more than if they had it there.

If you're on a budget, little things that you put thought into would mean a lot. A good idea is to do little things throughout the week. Leave a special something where she'll find it and maybe end the week with a nice dinner.

Remember, women like to be pursued. So if you do anything, help her see that if you could marry her all over again, you would.

Day 28

Don't Forget the Flowers, the Anniversary, or the Toothpaste

When my wife handed me the toothpaste I saw that she had squeezed it from the middle. "Who is this person? Toothpaste should always be squeezed from the bottom. Is she insane?"

Issues like this have always plagued marriages. Well, here are your solutions. Buy a stand-up toothpaste dispenser, mount your toilet paper roll vertically, and to end the toilet seat debate, put washers under the seat's rear mounting screws. This will tilt it, forever insuring its down position.

Do you ever ask your husband or wife to do a small task, and it's done with enthusiasm but forgotten two days later? The shouting probably begins here about how ten years ago your spouse neglected to think of you and now the wretched think-only-of-yourself sickness has obviously returned. You say things that you know you will regret, but you don't care and the quarrel ends with, "Why can't you ever think of someone besides yourself?"

Herein lies the root of many marital conflicts. You could remodel your whole bathroom, but the problem would manifest itself somewhere else because it's never really about toothpaste or toilet paper. Sometimes it's about how the car is parked, the dryness of the meatloaf, or the missing remote.

These miniscule items become notes in the divorce decree because one spouse does not believe that the other cares enough to do a simple task differently. When couples enter this mental state the very sight of their "loved one" sends them into a ranting tirade because, "You won't put the seat down!!"

You must keep in mind however that it's never about the task. It's about the missed anniversary, the door she has to get herself, and it's about never sending her flowers just because. Also, it's about not taking him some water when he's outside working, and it's about not pressing his shirt occasionally when it could really make his day.

Marital conflict consistently involves the other person's perception of what is happening. We all want to feel appreciated, loved, and desired and when we don't, we feel exactly the opposite and this isn't good for anyone.

I wasn't really irritated about the toothpaste I mentioned earlier because my wife is terribly cute. What's more important though is that she considers me throughout her day and I know she cares. When this sentiment is taken care of, the small stuff is just that; small and not worth our time.

Whether you are the absent-minded spouse or the fault-finder, make some deposits today because your morning rituals should not be a steel cage death match. Instead, they should be another portion of your day that you are able to share with someone special.

Conclusion

I hope that over the course of reading this material you have gained a better understanding of your spouse and of yourself. Marriages tend to waiver because they are not being nurtured and they aren't being nurtured because of work, kids, and from just being human. Your marriage can be incredibly exciting if you put in the effort to make it such.

Please check out my website and subscribe through Facebook, RSS, e-zine, Twitter, or email. Through my articles, I hope you'll find more resources to make your marriage all that it can be.

God bless,
Dale Sadler

www.DaleSadler.net

dale@dalesadler.net

Made in the USA
Coppell, TX
02 August 2024

35488587R00039